START-A-CRAFT

Christmas Crafts

Get started in a new craft with easy-to-follow

projects for beginners

ALISON JENKINS

APPLE

A QUINTET BOOK

Published by The Apple Press
6 Blundell Street
London N7 9BH

ISBN 1-84092-101-3

This book was designed and produced by
Quintet Publishing Limited
6 Blundell Street
London N7 9BH

Creative Director: Richard Dewing
Designer: James Lawrence
Photographer: Andrew Sydenham

Typeset in Great Britain by
Central Southern Typesetters, Eastbourne
Manufactured in Singapore by Eray Scan Pte Ltd
Printed in China by Leefung-Asco Printers Ltd

CONTENTS

INTRODUCTION

Christmas is a joyous time for sharing and celebration, for fun and festivity for all the family. Decorating the house ready for Christmas is an age-old tradition that is enjoyed with much enthusiasm today. Holly, ivy and natural forms have for centuries been used as embellishments for the festive season. However, the Christmas tree itself was popularized in Britain during the 19th century by Prince Albert, Queen Victoria's husband. Indeed, the Victorians took great delight in crafts of all kinds and used the Christmas celebration as an ideal opportunity to display their skills. During recent years Christmas has become a rather commercialized occasion. Shops are crammed with a vast array of readymade decorations, cards and gifts, and sadly many people have never experienced the joy and satisfaction of making their own special decorations and tokens. This year, create a Christmas to remember, using this book as your guide and inspiration.

The 13 projects contained in this book will teach you a variety of simple craft skills and imaginative ways of using them, from simple paper folding, paint effects and dough craft to stencilling, sewing and wreathmaking; projects using metal and wire are also included. Each project has a comprehensive equipment list, step-by-step instructions, patterns, templates and handy tips or alternative ideas. A wide variety of materials is featured, ranging from paper, card and fabric to metal, wire and natural forms. The crafts require different skill levels: some are simple enough for children to help with or to do by themselves whilst others are a little more complicated, but all of the projects are designed with the beginner in mind.

Learning a new craft is fun, an activity for you and all the family to enjoy, and also a wonderful opportunity to experiment and to use your imagination.

Happy Christmas!

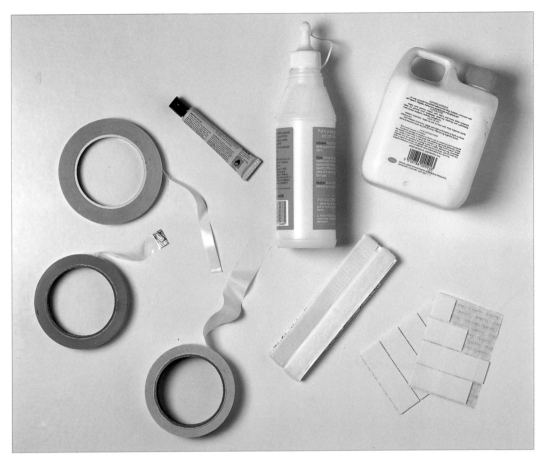

ADHESIVE TAPE AND GLUE

There are many different ways of fixing craft materials together. The success of your project often depends on choosing the correct one.

ADHESIVE TAPE. Double-sided tape is featured in many projects in this book. It is useful for fixing paper, card and fabric. Masking tape is low tack and is usually used for temporary fixing or for masking off areas. Clear tape can be used for paper or card but do not use it where the tape will be seen.

DOUBLE-SIDED ADHESIVE PADS. These are small foam pads with a strong adhesive on both sides, suitable for fixing most materials.

GLUE. Water-based glues are suitable for card and paper but you will need to use a stronger glue for fabric, beads or sequins. There are numerous specialist glues available for individual craft purposes, including those for metals and plastics.

VELCRO. This is a very clever form of fastening. The Velcro strip has lots of tiny loops on one side and hooks on the other; when pressed together, they hold quite firmly. Velcro is available in sew-in and self-adhesive form and a combination of both for use with paper, card and fabric.

PAINTING AND COLOURING EQUIPMENT

CRAFT PAINT. Acrylic paints are ideal for craft purposes, as they are quick drying and easily diluted. They can be cleaned up with water when wet but are permanent when dry.

SPRAY PAINT. Useful for painting delicate or intricate articles.

PENS AND PENCILS. Use soft pencils for sketching design lines or making tracings. Thick marker pens can be used for decorative purposes.

BRUSHES. Have a variety of brushes to apply both paint and glue. Always make sure to clean brushes thoroughly after use.

COCKTAIL STICKS AND SKEWERS. Useful for supporting craft items while they dry and for piercing holes, stirring paint and applying glue.

MIXING PALETTE. For mixing small quantities of paint or glue, though you can use an old saucer or dish for this.

SPIRAL PAPER GARLAND

Simple and colourful paper garlands to festoon the Christmas tree or decorate a room.
The garlands are most effective when made from two different coloured papers and can
easily be joined together to form longer strands. The folding method may be a little tricky at
first but once mastered is quick and easy to do. Children can help with this too.

1 Lay the sheets of paper on top of one another on a piece of thick card. (The card is used to protect your work surface from damage from the cutting blade.) Mark the cutting lines on the paper very lightly with a pencil about 1.5 cm (¾ in) apart. Then, using the scalpel or craft knife and the metal ruler, carefully cut the paper into strips.

2 Take two different coloured paper strips and place the ends together. Snip across the ends at an angle of 45 degrees.

You will need
◊ Large sheets of thin coloured paper
◊ Metal ruler
◊ Craft knife or scalpel
◊ Pencil
◊ Double-sided adhesive tape
◊ Thick sheet of card

SAFETY FIRST

• Always take extra care when using a sharp cutting blade or scalpel. Use a metal ruler as a guide to cutting straight lines and also to make sure that the blade doesn't slip.

3 Separate the two strips. Then turn the top strip over and fix to the first, using a small triangle of double-sided adhesive tape. The strips will form an inverted V shape.

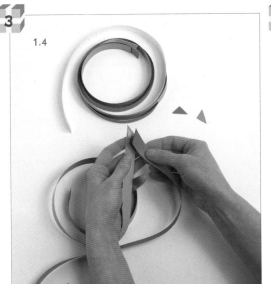

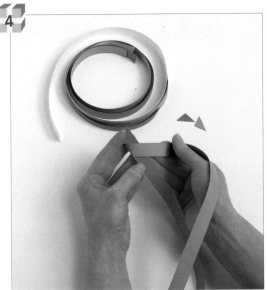

4 Carefully fold the first strip from left to right over the top strip. Press the fold firmly between your forefinger and thumb. Fold the second strip over the first in the same way, rotating the whole thing slightly clockwise as you go. Continue folding in this way.

5 As you fold, the strips will form a little hexagonal shape. As you continue, the spiral garland will be formed. When you reach the end of the paper strip, simply join on another, using a small piece of double-sided adhesive tape.

DECORATED GIFT WRAP

This year, wrap up the Christmas gifts in your own hand-decorated paper.
Plain matt poster paper can be transformed into a richly patterned and unusual gift wrap
using very simple paint techniques.

DAPPLED EFFECT PAPER

1 Lay the sheet of poster paper on a flat surface. Pour a small amount of gold paint onto a small saucer or mixing palette. Take a piece of tissue paper (you could use a piece of cloth) approximately 20 cm (8 in) square and crumple it up in your hand. Press the crumpled surface of the paper onto the paint in the saucer. Do not overload the paper with paint.

You will need
◊ Large sheets of plain matt poster paper
◊ Onion skin paper or tissue paper
◊ Scissors
◊ Ruler
◊ Masking tape
◊ Gold poster or acrylic craft paint
◊ Metallic gold spray paint
◊ Corrugated card to match poster paper

2 Press the paint-coated surface onto the poster paper to create the mottled pattern. Do this all over the paper, using a light dabbing action. Take care not to smudge the paint as you go.

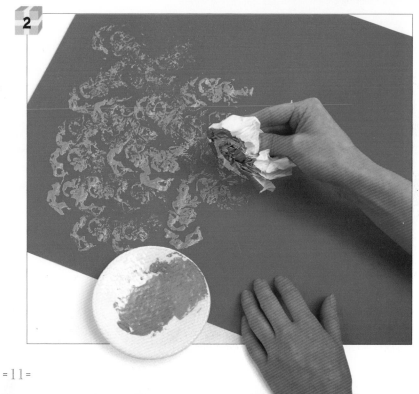

TIP
• Why not experiment with different coloured paints and background colours? Or use a combination of techniques to create your own individual patterns?

STRIPED EFFECT PAPER

1 Lay your poster paper on a flat surface and place masking tape in diagonal stripes about 2 cm (1 in) apart.

2 Apply gold paint, using the dappling technique described on page 11. Wait for the paint to dry a little before carefully removing the masking tape

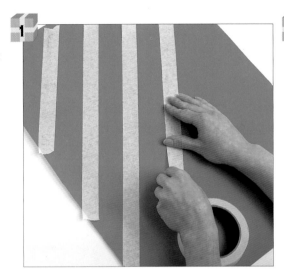

CHECK EFFECT

1 Take a sheet of poster paper and fold it up like a concertina or a fan. Make the folds about 1.5 cm (¾ in) wide. Stretch out the folded paper sheet a little and place it on your work surface. Using the metallic gold spray paint, coat the paper with a fine mist of colour. If you spray from one angle, only one side of the fold will catch the paint, creating a striped effect when the paper is opened out.

2 When the paint is dry, repeat the process but this time folding at right angles to the first folds. This creates a check effect.

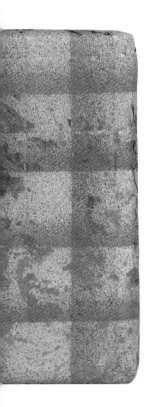

Add that special finishing touch with matching gift tags, pretty folded fans and strips of corrugated card.

SAFETY FIRST

• Always read instructions carefully when using spray paints. Use them only in a well-ventilated room. Protect or mask off other surfaces whilst spraying.

CHRISTMAS CRACKERS

These shiny Christmas crackers will ensure that your celebrations go with a bang!
Made from metallic-finish crepe paper, they add a touch of luxury to the Christmas dinner table.
Make one for each guest with a special gift inside.

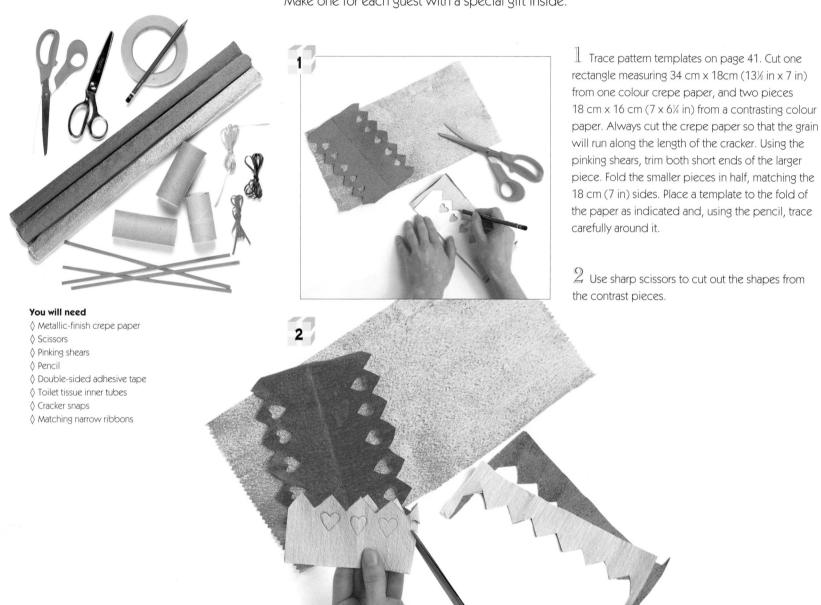

You will need

◊ Metallic-finish crepe paper
◊ Scissors
◊ Pinking shears
◊ Pencil
◊ Double-sided adhesive tape
◊ Toilet tissue inner tubes
◊ Cracker snaps
◊ Matching narrow ribbons

1 Trace pattern templates on page 41. Cut one rectangle measuring 34 cm x 18cm (13½ in x 7 in) from one colour crepe paper, and two pieces 18 cm x 16 cm (7 x 6¼ in) from a contrasting colour paper. Always cut the crepe paper so that the grain will run along the length of the cracker. Using the pinking shears, trim both short ends of the larger piece. Fold the smaller pieces in half, matching the 18 cm (7 in) sides. Place a template to the fold of the paper as indicated and, using the pencil, trace carefully around it.

2 Use sharp scissors to cut out the shapes from the contrast pieces.

3

3 Position the contrast cut-out pieces approximately 2 cm (1 in) in from the pinked edge of the larger rectangle. Fix in place with double-sided adhesive tape.

4

4 Take three cardboard inner tubes and trim one to approximately 11 cm (4½ in) long for the centre and the other two to 6 cm (2½ in) long for the ends. Turn the crepe paper piece over. Place the larger tube at the centre and the two smaller tubes about 1 cm (½ in) in from the pinked edge. Slip the cracker snap inside the cardboard tubes. Also at this point insert a small gift or some sweets into the centre tube. Wrap the crepe paper around the tubes.

5

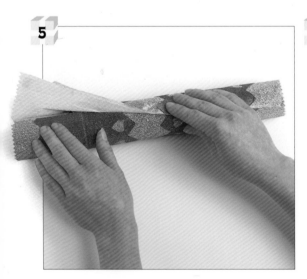

5 Fix the edge of the crepe paper firmly with a strip of double-sided adhesive tape.

6

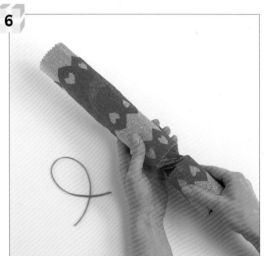

6 Hold the central part of the cracker with your left hand and one end with your right. Gently twist the cracker clockwise, then anticlockwise. This creases the paper between the cardboard tubes and makes it easier to tie in the next step.

7

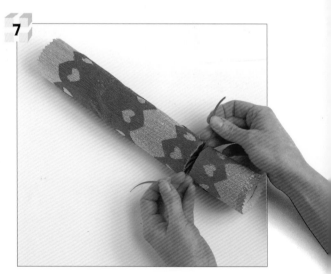

7 Take a short length of matching ribbon and tie the cracker tightly around the creased part. Trim off the ends of the ribbon. Tie the other end in the same way.

MINI CHRISTMAS TREES

A mini Christmas tree is ideal in many homes today where space is at a premium. Use the larger
tree to brighten up a small corner, the tiny ones to make your dinner table extra special.
A humble plantpot, some chicken wire and a few twigs are transformed with a spray of
gold paint and the addition of simple salt dough decorations and colourful ribbon trimmings.

You will need

◊ Chicken wire
◊ Small wire-cutter
◊ Terracotta flowerpots
◊ Dry bramble stalks or twigs
◊ Metallic gold spray paint
◊ Florists' oasis foam
◊ Knife
◊ Florists' wire
◊ Sphagnum moss
◊ Bundle of natural raffia
◊ Tartan ribbons
◊ Plain flour
◊ Salt
◊ Rolling pin
◊ Small star- and heart-shaped canapé cutters
◊ Double-sided adhesive tape

1 Using the wire-cutter, carefully cut out a
trapezium shape from the chicken wire. The
following measurements are approximate: larger
tree, depth 35.5 cm (14 in), base 55 cm (22 in),
top 25 cm (10 in), and for the smaller tree, depth
20.5 cm (8 in), base 30 cm (12 in), top 15 cm (6 in).

2 Bend the cut chicken wire
trapezium to form a cone shape.
Twist the wires together to join the
centre seam. Then snip off any untidy
ends with the wire-cutter.

SAFETY FIRST

• Always use spray paints in a well-ventilated
room. Protect work surfaces with
newspaper or a spare sheet of paper.
Follow instructions on the can carefully.
• Take care not to scratch or cut your hands
on the cut wire, as it can be quite sharp.

---

3 Take two dry bramble stalks or a few thin twigs
and tie them together with raffia. Spray the stalk, pot
and wire shape with metallic gold spray paint and
leave them to dry.

4

4 Cut a circle of florists' oasis foam to fit inside the pot snugly.

5

5 Place a small amount of sphagnum moss on top of the oasis foam. Fix it into place with small pieces of wire bent into U shapes.

6

6 Take three or four long strands of raffia and tie them together in a knot at the base of the wire tree shape. Wind the raffia in a spiral around the tree, tying securely at the top. Snip off any loose ends with scissors.

7

7 Using small pieces of tartan ribbon, tie the raffia to the wires at intervals all over the tree. Trim the ends of the ribbons into neat points.

8

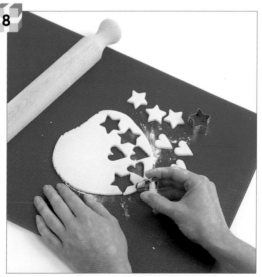

8 To make salt dough decorations, place eight tablespoons of plain flour and four of salt in a small bowl and mix into a dough with about eight tablespoons of water. Knead the dough until it is soft and pliable. Roll it out on a floured board to a thickness of about 5 mm (¼ in). Cut out little heart and star shapes, using the canapé cutters. Place the cut-out shapes on an oven tray and bake at 145°C/290°F/Gas Mark 1½ for about 1½ to 2 hours. If the shapes are not completely dry, leave them in a warm place overnight.

The larger tree has hanging shapes around the base edge. Simply pierce a small hole at the top of each shape with a bodkin or cocktail stock before they go into the oven. When the tree is finished, you can tie the shapes on with a small piece of raffia.

TIPS

- Use the dough recipe for making full-size tree decorations, using larger pastry cutters or trying your own shapes. Simply make a paper template and cut around the shape with a sharp knife.
- Salt dough can also be used to create flat and three-dimensional shapes for all sorts of other craft projects. Why not experiment a little?
- You can decorate your mini trees in a multitude of ways, with sequins and beads, pine cones or dry seed pods, dry leaves or flowers, dried fruit slices and nuts, paper cut-outs or even shiny foil-wrapped sweets.

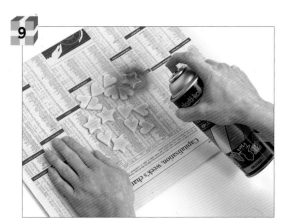

9 Spray the dough shapes on both sides with metallic gold paint and leave them to dry.

10 Fix the painted dough shapes to the tree, using small squares of double-sided adhesive tape.

11 Push the painted stalk firmly into the foam inside the pot, then place the tree over the stalk. You may need to squeeze the top edge together a little so that it stays in place.

CHRISTMAS WREATH

Nature has provided the basic materials for this delightful wreath. Holly, ivy and pine cones
are always in plentiful supply at this time of year. Hang the wreath on your front door or
use it as a table centrepiece with candles to celebrate the festive season.

You will need

◊ Long strands of variegated ivy
◊ Sprigs of holly
◊ Pine cones
◊ Small wire-cutters
◊ Florists' wire

1 Taking two long strands of ivy, wind them
loosely around each other to form a circle about
30 cm (12 in) in diameter.

2 Wind another three or four strands of ivy around
the base, tucking in the ends neatly as you go.

3 Trim the holly sprigs to about 18 cm (7 in) long.
Push the stems into the ivy base around the outside.
Fix the holly in place with short lengths of wire if this
seems to be necessary. Take care not to scratch your
hands: the holly prickles can be very sharp!

4 Finally, wind a short length of wire around the base of each pine cone, leaving two prongs protruding downwards. If the cones are open, this should be quite easy to do.

5 Fix each pine cone to the inside of the ivy base by pushing the wire prongs into the ivy base and twisting them together at the back, making them secure.

TABLE DECORATION

Make a table decoration that is both attractive and edible. A cannel knife is used to engrave patterns into the skin of small clementines. The designs used here are very simple, but why not experiment a little with your own designs or use larger fruits with more surface area to decorate?

You will need

◊ 7 small, firm-skinned clementines
◊ Cannel knife
◊ Block of florists' oasis foam for dry arrangements
◊ Whole cloves
◊ Florists' wire
◊ Small wire-cutter
◊ Small sprigs of fresh green foliage
◊ Large slow-burning candle

1 Hold a clementine firmly in one hand and the cannel knife in the other. Beginning at the centre of the fruit, press the knife gently into the skin, making vertical lines down the sides. As you drag the knife along, it will cut a shallow groove in the skin to reveal the white pith underneath. You may need to practise a little before you begin the finished piece. Make about eight grooves in each fruit. Engrave three clementines in this way.

2 For the spiral patterns, hold the fruit in one hand and the knife in the other as before. Press the knife into the skin at the centre, then gently rotate the fruit anticlockwise, cutting a continuous groove around the fruit. Engrave four clementines in this way.

3 Cut the oasis foam into a circle approximately 10 cm (4 in) in diameter and 5 cm (2 in) deep.

TIPS

• After engraving the fruits, keep the narrow strips of skin, dry them and use them to add colour and citrus fragrance to pot-pourri.
• Engrave larger citrus fruits, such as oranges, in the same way. Use them as a table centrepiece, piled up in a large bowl. Your guests can eat them after dinner!

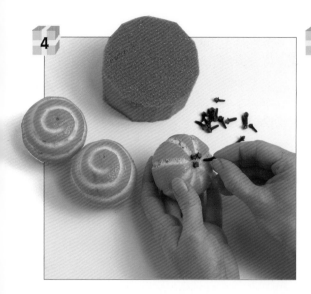

4 Carefully press whole cloves into the centres of the fruits. This gives a lovely fragrance in addition to decorative effect.

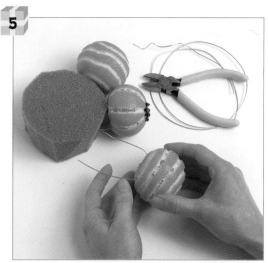

5 Using the wire-cutter, cut a 15 cm (6 in) piece of wire for each fruit. Push the wire through the base of each fruit and bend to form a U shape. Then push the ends of the wire into the foam base.

6 Trim some fresh green foliage, such as holly or another evergreen, into small sprigs. Push the stems firmly into the oasis foam.

7 Press the base of the candle into the centre of the foam base.

SAFETY FIRST

• Never leave a burning candle unattended. Always place decorations containing candles on a heat-proof surface.

GIFT BAGS

These charming country-look gift bags make perfect containers for Christmas presents.

You will need
◊ Thin white card
◊ Thin coloured card
◊ Paper or card with a surface texture
◊ Check cotton fabric
◊ Pencil
◊ Ruler
◊ Knife
◊ Scissors

◊ Water-based glue suitable for fabric and paper
◊ Paint brush
◊ Double-sided adhesive tape
◊ Leather punch
◊ Ball of string
◊ Small buttons with two holes

1 Trace the template given on page 42, transferring all the fold lines accurately. The template shows the two sizes. For the bag made of card, cut out a box shape in coloured or textured card; for the fabric-covered bag, use thin white card. Score along all the dotted lines.

2 For the fabric-covered bag, cut a piece of fabric about 2 cm (1 in) larger all round than the card shape. Glue the shape to the fabric and smooth out any air bubbles. Trim the fabric close to the card shape, leaving the 2 cm (1 in) excess at the upper edge. Crease at the fold positions again.

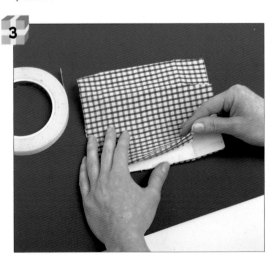

3 Fix the tab to the side edge using double-sided adhesive tape.

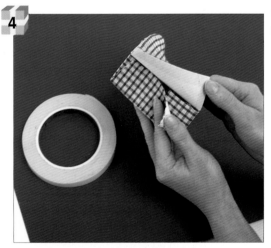

4 Fold in the flaps at the lower edge to form the base of the bag. Fix in place using double-sided adhesive tape.

5 Apply a strip of double-sided tape to the inside of the bag around the upper edge. For the fabric-covered bag, fold down the fabric neatly.

6

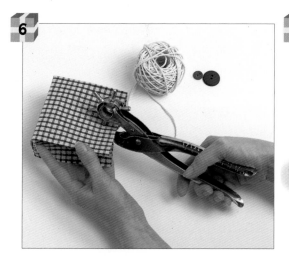

6 For the fastening, use the leather punch to pierce a hole at the centre of the bag, about 1.5 cm (¾ in) down from the folded edge.

7

7 To make button fastenings, first cut a 25 cm (10 in) piece of string for each. Fold the string in half, then pass the ends through the holes in the button and tie in a knot. Next, pass the loop end through the punched holes at the top of the bag, then bring the loop around the button at the front. This makes a very pretty and secure fastening for your gift bag.

8

8 To make a fish gift tag, trace the tag template given on page 42. Cut one shape from thin coloured card. Score and fold it along the dotted line. Pierce a small hole at the head end, using the paper punch. Glue on a small button for the eye. Knot on a short length of string and tie up the gift bag with a neat little bow.

9

9 To make fish and heart decorations, trace the fish and heart motifs given on page 42. Cut them out in fabric or card and fix them to the front of the bag with glue or double-sided tape.

TIP

• The template for these gift bags shows two sizes, but if you require a smaller or larger gift bag, simply enlarge or reduce the original on a photocopying machine.

TREE DECORATIONS

Forget expensive, shop-bought tree decorations this year! Make your own from some string and a few polystyrene shapes. Ours are linked together with golden beads and tassels and have tiny star sequins that will catch the light and twinkle beautifully on your Christmas tree.

You will need

◊ Polystyrene craft balls
◊ Ball of string
◊ Water-based glue
◊ Quick-drying craft glue
◊ Paint brush
◊ Scissors
◊ Quick-drying acrylic paint
  (base colour and metallic gold)
◊ Cocktail sticks
◊ Plasticine
◊ Small sponge
◊ Gold beads and sequins
◊ Sewing thread
◊ Bodkin
◊ Gold thread
◊ Gold tassels

1 Place the polystyrene ball on the end of a cocktail stick. This is a useful way of holding the ball steady whilst glueing and painting. Coat the polystyrene ball with a water-based craft glue. (Other glues melt the polystyrene.) Take the end of the string and wind it around the cocktail stick at the base of the ball. Slowly rotate the ball, winding the string around as you go. The string will stick to the tacky surface of the glue. Snip off the string when you reach the top. Use the plasticine to keep the string-covered shapes upright as they dry.

2 For the flat, round shapes, take a piece of string about 30 cm (12 in) long and coat it with glue. Coil it up from the centre and leave it to dry.

3 Apply one or two coats of acrylic paint to each shape. Acrylic paint is ideal for craft purposes as it dries quickly.

TIP

• If you can't find polystyrene balls, you could revamp old tree decorations by glueing string to the outside, or perhaps use an old pingpong ball for the small sizes. For a different shape, you could try using a blown egg.

4

5

6

4 Pour a little of the metallic gold paint onto a small saucer or mixing palette. Take a small piece of sponge and dip it into the paint. Use a light dabbing motion to transfer the gold paint to the string-covered shapes.

5 When the paint has dried, use a quick-drying craft glue to apply tiny gold star sequins at random over the shapes. First squeeze a tiny spot of glue onto the shape, then pick up the sequin on the end of your finger and place it gently onto the glue spot.

6 In assembling the decorations, use your imagination to create unusual effects with different combinations of round and flat shapes, together with beads and tassels. First thread some beads or a tassel onto matching sewing thread. Attach the thread to a thicker gold thread loop. Make this loop long enough to go through the ball and leave enough to hang it by at the top. Thread the loop onto a long bodkin. The polystyrene is soft enough for the bodkin to pass through quite easily. If you have any difficulty, pierce the ball with a skewer or a thin knitting needle first.

PARTY HATS

Dazzling hats to put everyone in the party mood. Two colours of reflective mirror card are combined effectively, using simple shapes and a clever woven detail.

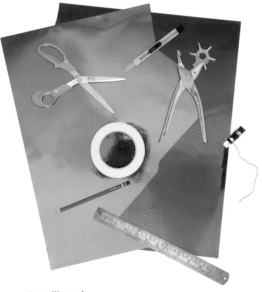

You will need
◊ Sheets of metallic mirrorcard in two colours
◊ Pencil
◊ Metal ruler
◊ Scalpel or sharp craft knife
◊ Scissors
◊ Leather punch
◊ Double-sided adhesive tape
◊ Shirring elastic

1 Trace the hat and star templates given on page 43. Transfer the tracings to the wrong side of the metallic card, making sure to mark all the cutting lines accurately. Cut them out carefully, using the scissors. Cut the hat shape and the star from different colours.

2 Cut the V-shaped lines of the woven detail, using a sharp craft knife and a metal ruler.

3 Take a hat shape and a star and begin to weave by first slotting point 3 under C, then point 2 under B, then point 3 under A. Slide the shapes together as far as they will go.

4 Lift up point 2 and tuck point C underneath it. Then lift up point 1 and tuck point B underneath.

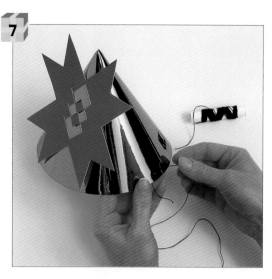

5 Finally, bring point C over point 1 to complete the woven detail.

6 Using the leather punch, pierce a small hole either side of the hat shape. The position is indicated on the template. Apply a strip of double-sided adhesive tape to the tab area.

7 Tear the backing paper from the tape and fix the hat into a cone shape. Thread a 35 cm (14 in) piece of shirring elastic through the pierced holes at each side of the hat and tie securely in a knot.

TIPS

- Why not use the hats as party invitations? Send the hats to each of your guests, flat in a large envelope, with the party invitation written on the back.
- The woven detail on the hat is a simple but effective way of joining two pieces of card or paper together.
- You could apply the star motif to a square or rectangular piece and use it as a greetings card. Also, using the V-shaped cuts and the same method, you could create your own shapes.

STENCILLED INVITATIONS AND PLACE CARDS

Gold on ivory is a stylish colour combination for these matching invitations and place cards.
This project offers four different designs for you to choose from, each requiring a different skill level.

You will need

◊ Clear acetate stencil film
◊ Pencil
◊ Scalpel or swivel-blade craft knife
◊ Leather punch
◊ Textured paper, such as a heavyweight watercolour paper
◊ Gold stencil paint
◊ Sponge
◊ Ruler
◊ Scoring knife
◊ Sharp craft knife
◊ Metallic writing pen

STENCILS

1 Trace the stencil templates given on page 44. Place the traced design on a thick card sheet or a safe cutting surface and place a rectangle of acetate the same size on top. Use tabs of masking tape to keep the acetate in place. Carefully cut out the design, using your scalpel or swivel-blade craft knife. The star and heart are the easiest ones to start with. The holly involves more curved lines. The gift is a little more difficult. For the gift, cut out only the ribbon at this first stage.

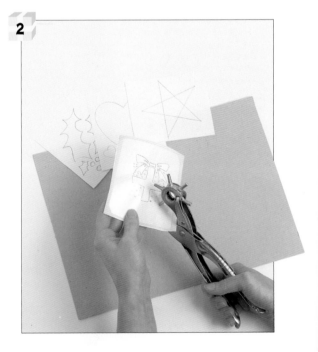

2 Use the leather punch to cut the tiny dots on the gift stencil. These would be too difficult to cut with a blade.

INVITATION

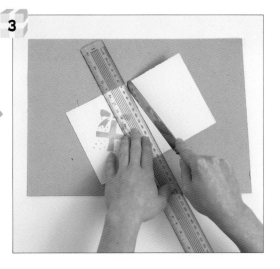

1 Cut a rectangle of paper measuring 20 cm x 12 cm (8 in x 4¾ in) for each invitation. Mark the halfway point lightly with a pencil line. Place the stencil in the centre of the lefthand portion. Pour a little of the gold stencil paint onto a small saucer or mixing palette. Take a small piece of sponge and press the surface onto the paint. Do not overload the sponge with paint: only a small amount is needed. Now press the sponge lightly onto the stencil using a dabbing action. Stencilling is very easy when you get the hang of it, but practise on a sheet of spare paper if you are unsure. Allow the paint to dry a little and then remove the stencil carefully.

2 Beginning at the top of the stencilled pattern, halfway across the front portion of the paper, use the scalpel to cut carefully around the righthand side of the design. Stop when you reach the bottom, again about halfway across the front portion.

3 Using a ruler and a blunt knife, score along the halfway point. Then score halfway across the front portion, above and below the stencilled design, not across the design itself.

PLACE CARDS

Cut a square of paper measuring 12 cm x 12 cm (4¾ in x 4¾ in) for each place card. Mark the halfway point, then stencil the design as before but positioning the stencil slightly to the left of centre. Score across the halfway point, again avoiding the stencilled design itself. Write a name on the card with a metallic gold pen and then fold as shown.

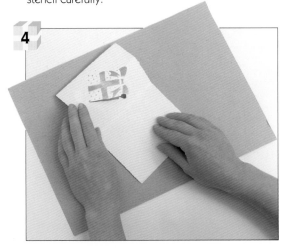

4 Fold along the score lines as shown, so the stencilled design stands out of the folded front part. This gives a very simple 3D effect.

CHRISTMAS CARDS

Send your special Christmas greetings this year inside these unusual cards made from pieces of an old tin can! They're fun to make, and a card made by hand is always a joy to receive.

You will need

◊ Sheets of thin coloured card, some with
   surface texture
◊ Pencil
◊ Ruler
◊ Scoring knife
◊ Scalpel or sharp craft knife
◊ Pieces of tin
◊ Small hammer
◊ Centre punch
◊ Double-sided adhesive tape
◊ Masking tape
◊ Tin snip
◊ Protective gloves
◊ Hessian fabric
◊ Double-sided adhesive pads

The metal pieces we used came from the side of a large empty coffee tin. Use the tin snip to remove the top and base of the tin, then cut down the side and open up the tin to form a flat sheet.

SAFETY FIRST

• Always use protective gloves when cutting metal,
  as the edges can be very sharp.
• When punching out the designs, use a thick card
  sheet to protect your work surface.

FRAMED MOTIF CARD

1 Trace the card templates and motif outlines given on pages 45-46 (templates given for square, rectangular and triangular cards). Make sure to transfer all cutting lines and fold lines accurately. The dots on the motif outlines indicate the punch hole positions. Cut the basic card shape, then cut out the window, using a scalpel and a metal ruler. Score and fold where indicated.

2 Choose a motif for your card, then cut a piece of tin about 2 cm (1 in) larger than the motif all round. Place the metal piece on a thick card sheet, then place the traced motif on top. Hold the tracing in place with tabs of masking tape. Next, begin to punch along the dotted lines of the traced motif. Place the point of the centre punch on each dot and tap once or twice with the hammer. The aim is to make a clear dent in the surface of the metal, not to pierce a hole right through. Continue until the motif is complete, then remove the tracing.

3 Using the tin snip, trim the metal piece so it is 1 cm (⅛ in) larger than the window in the central portion of the card. Fix the metal face down behind the window, using double-sided adhesive tape.

4 Fold the lefthand portion of the card over the centre to cover the back of the metal piece. Fix it in place with double-sided adhesive tape.

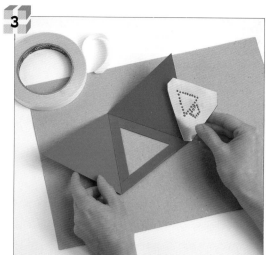

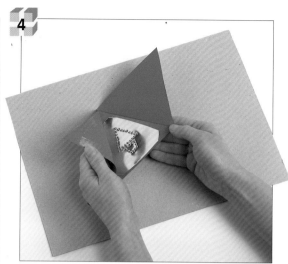

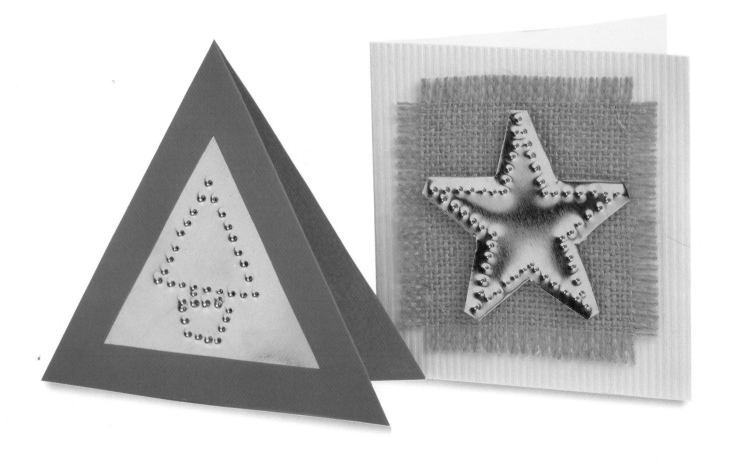

CUT-OUT MOTIF-CARD

1 Cut out the basic card shape but do not cut out the window. Score and fold where indicated and make up the card as before. Cut a piece of hessian about 5 cm x 5 cm (2 in x 2 in) and fray the edges. Choose a motif and punch out the design as before, then trim around the edge of the design, using the tin snip.

2 Fix the hessian square to the front of the card with double-sided adhesive tape. Fix the metal cut-out motif to the centre with double-sided adhesive pads.

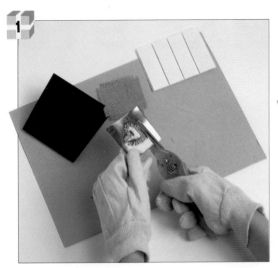

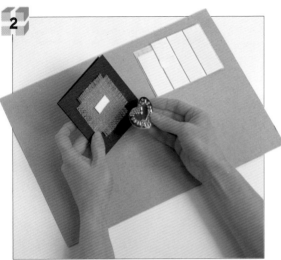

TIP

• If you cannot obtain suitable metal pieces, the same method can be used to punch design into metallic-finish card.

CHRISTMAS STOCKINGS

Jolly Christmas stockings ready to hang up on Christmas Eve. This project involves basic sewing skills only, but the use of the eyelets and glossy satin ribbons lends that professional touch. The stockings are washable and you'll be able to use them year after year.

You will need

◊ 50 cm (20 in) taffeta fabric
◊ 50 cm (20 in) lightweight polyester wadding
◊ 50 cm (20 in) red taffeta lining
◊ Scissors
◊ Pins
◊ 130 cm (51 in) narrow black satin binding
◊ Sewing needles
◊ Sewing thread
◊ Gilt eyelet kit (10 eyelets for each stocking)
◊ Hammer
◊ Flat piece of wood
◊ 1 m (39 in) red satin ribbon
◊ Sewing machine (optional)

The fabric and binding amounts are for each stocking.

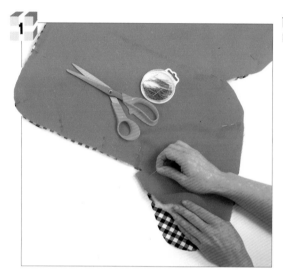

1 Trace the stocking pattern given on page 47 to full size. Place pattern to the fold of the fabric as indicated. Cut out one pattern each in fabric, wadding and lining. Pin the layers together, sandwiching the wadding between the fabric and lining.

3 Wrap the binding around the raw edge and slip-stitch the fold by hand to the original stitching line. Try to keep the stitches as small as possible.

2 Open the satin binding out slightly. Pin the right side of the binding to the lining side of the stocking around the front and upper edges, matching the raw edge of the binding to the raw edge of the stocking. Take care to ease the binding around the curves. Pin regularly at intervals of about 2 cm (1 in). Machine stitch the binding in place or, if you don't have a sewing machine, hand sew the binding using a small running stitch. Try to stitch on the fold of the binding that is closest to the raw edge.

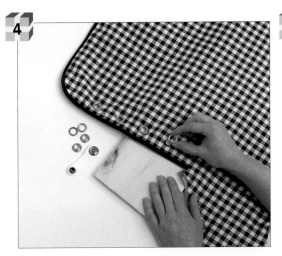

4 Insert eyelets in the positions marked in your pattern. (There will be instructions included in the eyelet kit.) First place the stocking on a hard surface, such as a piece of wood. Use the tool provided in the kit to make a hole at the position marked. Place the back piece under the hole and gently press through, then place the top part over the first.

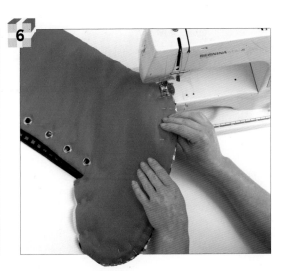

5 Place the tool over the eyelet, and hammer the pieces together.

6 Fold the stocking in half along the centre back seam. Then stitch the curved foot seam together, taking a seam allowance of about 1.5 cm (¾ in). Again, if you do not have a sewing machine, this can be done by hand, using a small running stitch.

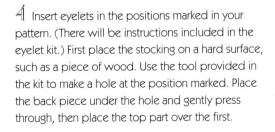

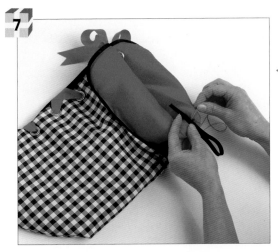

7 Turn the stocking through to the right side and thread the satin ribbon through the eyelets, finishing off with a neat bow at the top. For the hanging loop, take a further 20 cm (8 in) of binding, fold it in half and stitch along the length. Then fold in half to form a loop and stitch to the inside of the stocking at the centre back.

ADVENT CALENDAR

Children will love this Christmas tree Advent calendar, complete with shining star, a host of chirpy robins and a pile of little gifts. Each one hides a box containing sweets or a small surprise and has a number to correspond to each of the days up to Christmas.

You will need

◊ Stiff card (green, white and red)
◊ Pencil
◊ Scissors
◊ Double-sided adhesive tape
◊ Double-sided adhesive pads
◊ Assorted scraps of paper (brown, red, black, gold etc)
◊ Scraps of corrugated card (red, green)
◊ Narrow ribbons (assorted colours)
◊ Craft knife
◊ Double-sided adhesive Velcro fastening
◊ Adhesive numbers

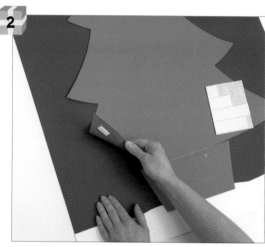

1 To make the tree and background, trace the pattern pieces full size, using the grid given on page 47. (Each square represents 5 cm (2 in).) First cut out the snow from the white card and use double-sided tape to fix it in place on the large blue background board. Then cut out the pot from red card and the tree from green.

2 Fix the tree and the pot to the background, using double-sided adhesive pads. This will give a slightly three-dimensional effect.

3 To make the robins, trace the robin template shapes given on page 48. You will need to make 12 robins. Cut the main body in brown, the wings in black and the chest in red. Remember that the robins need to face each other, so make six that look to the left and six that look to the right.

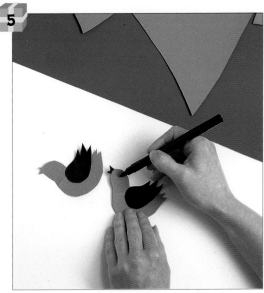

4 Assemble the robins, using double-sided adhesive tape.

5 When the robins are complete, draw in the eyes with a dark pen.

6 To make the boxes, trace the box tray and sleeve templates given on page 48. Cut 24 trays in white card, 13 sleeves in green card and 11 sleeves in white. Score and fold where indicated. Make up the box trays and fix with double-sided tape.

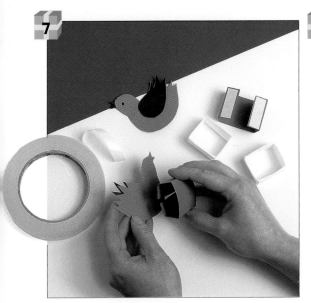

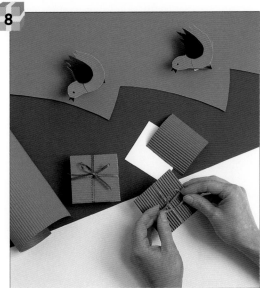

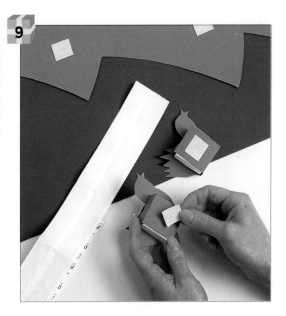

7 Using double-sided tape, fix the green sleeves as shown to the back of the robins and the star, and save the white ones to fix onto the gifts (step 8).

8 To make the gifts, cut six squares 7 cm x 7 cm (2¾ in x 2¾ in) and five rectangles 5 cm x 7 cm (2 in x 2¾ in) from stiff white card. Cover the squares and rectangles with scraps of corrugated card, paper, foil or wrapping paper, then tie each with a ribbon bow. Attach a box to the back of each gift as before.

9 Cut 24 pieces of Velcro, each 2 cm (⅞ in) long. Separate the hook side from the loop side and fix one to the back of each box sleeve and the other to the calendar. Use the photograph as a guide to positioning.

10 Trace the star template given on page 48. Cut out the star in gold card and fix a box to the back.

11 Stick a number on each of the robins and the gifts but make the star number 24. Fix each piece into place on the calendar, and then count the days to Christmas!

TEMPLATES

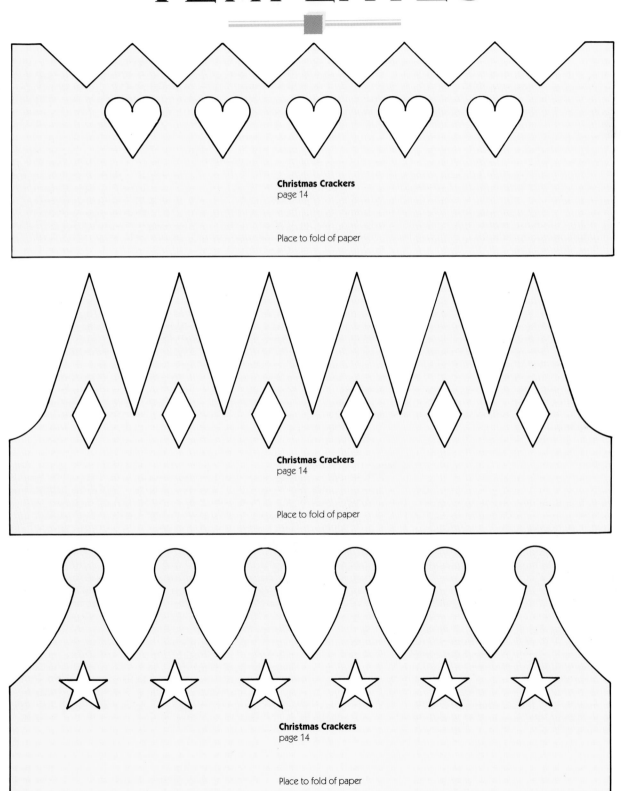

Christmas Crackers
page 14

Place to fold of paper

Christmas Crackers
page 14

Place to fold of paper

Christmas Crackers
page 14

Place to fold of paper

Large Bag

Small Bag

Gift Bags
page 24 (2 sizes)

Cut along solid lines
Score and fold along dotted lines

Tab

Gift Bag Heart Motif

Fold

Gift Bag Fish Tag

Gift Bag Fish Motif

Party Hat (Base)
page 28

Side Edge

C

B

A

**Party Hat
(Star Motif)**
page 28

1

2

3

Stencilled Invitations and Place Cards
page 30

Heart

Star

Holly

Gift

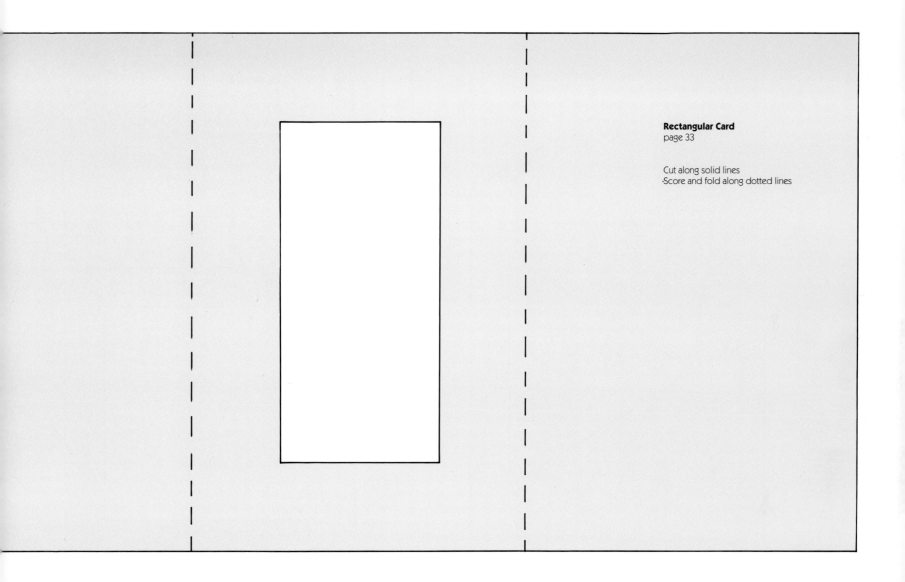

Rectangular Card
page 33

Cut along solid lines
·Score and fold along dotted lines

**Christmas Cards
(Punched Tin Motifs)**
page 33

Dots show punch holes

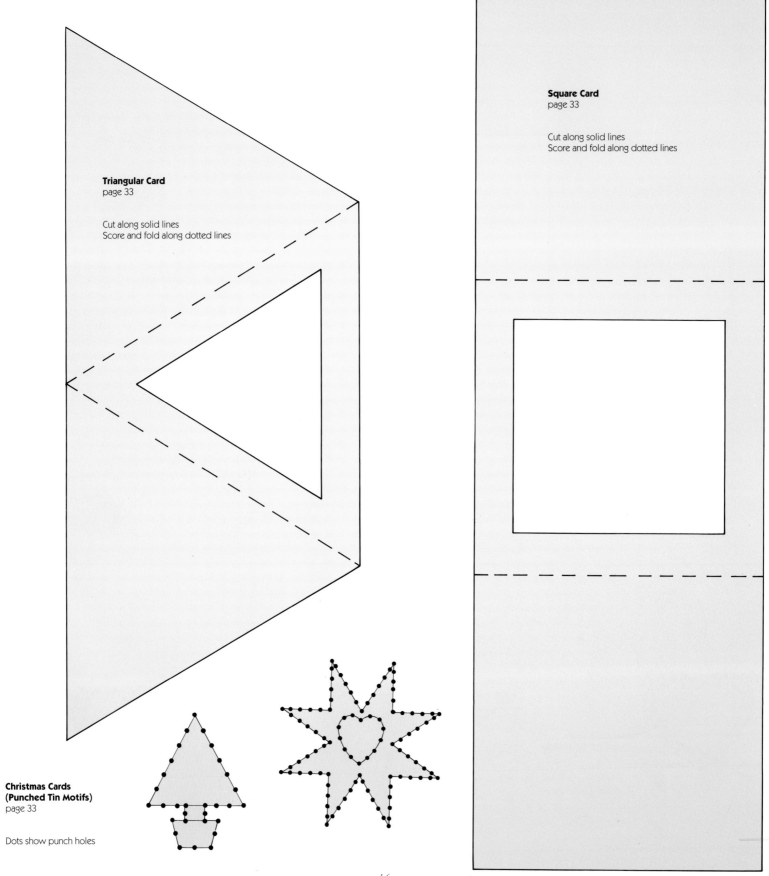

Triangular Card
page 33

Cut along solid lines
Score and fold along dotted lines

Square Card
page 33

Cut along solid lines
Score and fold along dotted lines

**Christmas Cards
(Punched Tin Motifs)**
page 33

Dots show punch holes

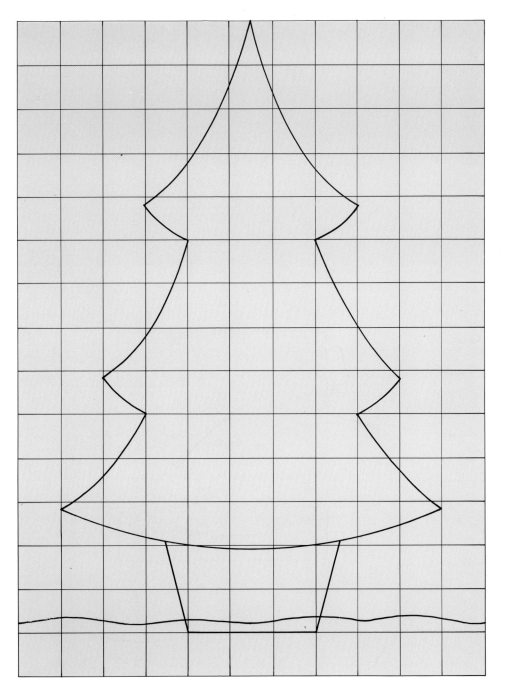

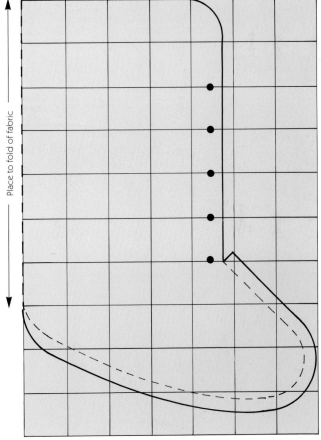

Christmas Tree Advent Calendar (Tree)
page 38
Each square represents 5 cm (2 in)

Christmas Stocking
page 36
Each square represents 5 cm (2 in)
Pattern includes 1.5 cm (¾ in) seam allowance around foot seam
Dots indicate eyelet position
Cut a piece each for fabric, lining and wadding

Place to fold of fabric

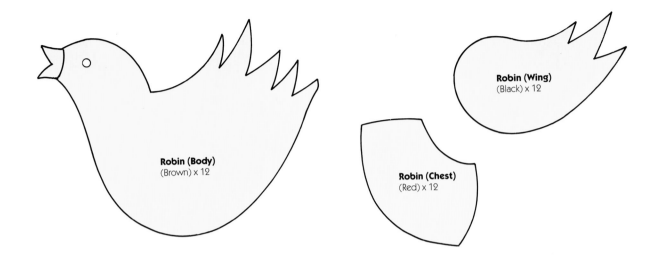

Robin (Body)
(Brown) x 12

Robin (Chest)
(Red) x 12

Robin (Wing)
(Black) x 12

**Christmas Tree Advent
Calendar (Motifs)**
page 38-40

**Christmas Tree Advent
Calendar (Boxes)**
page 39

Cut along solid lines
Score and fold along dotted lines

Star x 1

Box Tray

Box Sleeve